KEVIN McHALE

★

MICHAEL JORDAN

Jordan Deutsch

AVON   SUPERSTARS

AVON BOOKS
A division of
The Hearst Corporation
1790 Broadway
New York, New York 10019

Copyright © 1987 by Avon Books
Published by arrangement with the author
ISBN: 0-380-75312-X

Cover photos: McHale—Noren Trotman/SportsChrome;
Jordan—Focus on Sports

All rights reserved, which includes the right to reproduce this book or portions thereof in any form whatsoever except as provided by the U.S. Coyright Law. For information address Avon Books.

First Avon Printing: February 1987

AVON TRADEMARK REG. U.S. PAT. OFF. AND IN OTHER COUNTRIES, MARCA REGISTRADA, HECHO EN U.S.A.

Printed in the U.S.A.

OPM   10   9   8   7   6   5   4   3   2   1

Avon Books are available at special quantity discounts for bulk purchases for sales promotions, premiums, fund raising or educational use. Special books, or book excerpts, can also be created to fit specific needs.

For details write or telephone the office of the Director of Special Markets, Avon Books, Dept. FP, 1790 Broadway, New York, New York 10019, 212-399-1357.

KEVIN MCHALE

1
Destined to Play Basketball!

Whatever Kevin Edward McHale cooks up, he's sure to add a little spice. Take his birth, for example. Although he probably had little to do with choosing the time, it just happened to come six days before Christmas 1957. The exact date was December 19, when the shopping at the stores is at a frantic pace. For his parents, Paul and Josephine, it was the biggest gift they could get. But little did they know that *big* really meant *gigantic*! After all, Paul was an average 5 feet 10 inches and Kevin's mother was 5 feet 6 inches, heights that Kevin would pass before his tenth birthday! Oddly enough, his older brother, John, "only" grew to 6 feet, 1 inch, and his younger sisters, Patricia and Mary, also wound up under the six-foot mark. Kevin, though, would keep going until he had reached 6 feet 11 inches.

The town where Kevin was born was Hibbing, in northern Minnesota, which is the heart of what is known as the "Iron Range." It's the place where a lot of the ore to make steel comes from. Kevin's father, in fact, worked as an Iron Ranger for U.S. Steel for forty-two years before retiring in 1982. As part of his job, he would help load ore into railroad cars bound for Pittsburgh and Detroit.

Northern Minnesota is also "hockey country"

and Kevin, like many boys growing up in that part of the country, had one goal in mind: playing in the National Hockey League. There was nothing more exciting for Kevin than charging down the ice and blasting the puck into the net. But then one day a funny thing happened—strange enough for Kevin to forget about becoming a hockey player and instead concentrate on what his body was trying to tell him. He was in the ninth grade and already 6 feet 6 inches tall! When a charging defenseman decided to go *through* Kevin's legs instead of around him, he knew it was time to hang up his skates.

The next year he became serious about the game that would eventually bring him a roomful of trophies and millions of dollars. As Kevin tells it, "In the ninth grade I was just average at every sport I tried. I was always so awkward, I could never get anything flowing in the same direction. But by sophomore year, basketball was all I wanted to do because I became more and more successful at it. It was a snowball effect.

"I was blessed with this body for basketball. My parents aren't that tall and neither is my brother. It was me, so I have to use the gift to my best advantage."

Kevin went to Hibbing High and there met Gary Addington, the basketball coach who was to have a great influence on his development. Addington, seeing Kevin's determination, decided to work with him by playing game after game of one-on-one. The one exception to the rules was that Kevin was not allowed to use the lane. After all, the coach was only 6 feet 1. But he had another reason, too. He knew that Kevin would have no problem under the boards, but outside was a different story. So he wanted to help Kevin develop by forcing him to concentrate on his weaknesses. The loser had to buy milkshakes.

Even when it came to the actual games, Addington would not let him play the low post right near the basket. It was a move that Kevin would later really appreciate. As he says, "I would have gotten into a rut, scoring 30 points a game with my back to the basket. But Gary forced me to learn the whole game."

While Kevin was sharpening his skills on the court, he was also getting his teammates to laugh. Whenever the team did wind sprints during practice, they would refer to it as Garmakers, named after Dick Garmaker, an all-star guard with the Lakers and the Knicks in the 1950s, who just happened to be the only NBA player to come from Hibbing before McHale. What did Kevin think of "Garmakers"? "I've always associated the guy with a lot of pain."

Hibbing, by the way, produced another great talent, although not in the sports world: Bob Dylan, the legendary folk-rock singer, comes from the small Minnesota town. It just might be why Kevin names Dylan as his favorite singer.

By the time Kevin was a senior at Hibbing High his basketball reputation was spreading throughout the state. His height had shot up to 6 feet 10 inches and he was dominating most of the games he played. By now, having learned to score effectively from the outside, Coach Addington's prodigy was allowed to play down low. It was a move that brought the Blue Jackets to the state finals.

When it came to selecting a college, Kevin and his family decided to stay loyal to the state, selecting the University of Minnesota, in the twin cities of Minneapolis and St. Paul.

The competition in high school had been a snap compared to what he would be facing at Minnesota, which was part of the tough Big Ten Conference.

2

From the Gophers to the Celtics

When Kevin McHale showed up at the Minnesota University gym in the fall of 1976, his general appearance made a lasting impression on friend and teammate Phil Sanders: "When he came to school here he was just a long-legged, gangly kid. He was barrel-chested, and knock-kneed. He looked like Herman Munster—a reference to the TV comedy featuring a Frankenstein look-alike. It was McHale's unusual build that *Boston Globe* writer Dan Shaughnessy would later say was responsible for much of Kevin's success. Shaughnessy also supplied the best description of that "unusual build" when he wrote, "He looks like someone who either cannot exhale or has a coat-hanger underneath his shirt. His shoulders are pinned back, his chest heaves forward, and his arms dangle down around his knees."

It is McHale's arms, which measure an impressive 40 inches, that cause so much trouble for the opposition. But before he could show head coach Jim Dutchert what those arms—and the rest of him—could do, Kevin had to take a spot on the bench with the other freshmen. As fate would have it though, Kevin didn't stay on the bench for long. Even before the season started, he found himself on the starting lineup: a forward got injured and Kevin was sent in to take his place. This was at the Pillsbury Classic, a preseason tournament that no longer exists. Kevin's abilities would be greatly sharpened by Dutchert during his college days, but even this early on, he played well enough to lead Minnesota, known as the Gophers, to the tournament title and be named the tournament MVP!

After his great play in the Pillsbury Classic, he became a permanent fixture on the starting five, playing forward alongside center Mychal Thompson, now with the Portland Trail Blazers. By the time the season ended, Kevin was beginning to show some of the defensive ability that would make him such a great player. He took down 218 rebounds for the Gophers and helped lead the team to a 24–3 record. In between his studies and basketball, Kevin also found time to play golf and backgammon and, of course, to fish and hunt.

It seemed that all the attention he was getting wasn't affecting him at all. He was still the easygoing countryboy or, as he is still described, "an overgrown kid who would be just as happy to go hunting and fishing." To know how relaxed and down-to-earth Kevin was—and still is—you only have to listen to Sanders, who went on to become assistant coach under Dutchert: "Kevin's so easygoing, you could probably talk him into letting you drive off with his truck."

Maybe, but it's doubtful that his wife, Lynn, would allow Kevin to be so charitable. After all, who outside his family could know Kevin as well? Lynn, also from Hibbing, just happens to be McHale's childhood sweetheart.

Kevin's second year at Minnesota was still a time for improving his game. But even playing as he did, he couldn't lead the Gophers beyond their 17–10 overall record and a second-place finish in the Big Ten with a 12–6 mark. In fact, even individual recognition did not come for McHale until his junior year at Minnesota. By then, his play had improved to the point where he was named All–Big Ten and the team MVP! His 259 rebounds were enough to convince Indiana head coach Bobby Knight to take Kevin to the Pan American Games, held that year (1979) in Puerto Rico, where Kevin helped to lead the U.S.A. team to the gold medal. For McHale, as for the other college basketball stars who have been fortunate enough to play under the fiery coach, it was an "educating experience," but not, as Kevin said, one that he would "want for four years." They are, however, still good friends.

Aside from roaming the Minnesota woods and casting his line in the water, Kevin also spent part of the summer, as he had done the previous two summers, working alongside his father as an Iron Ranger. It was an experience that got him even closer to his dad; as Kevin says with great enthusiasm, "Paul A. McHale, my dad, is my Main Man." Working in the fields not only helped keep Kevin in top physical condition but provided the money for extras such as the odd-sized clothes he couldn't always find at the local shops in Hibbing. It also gave him a greater appreciation of what it could mean to play basketball for a living, which he later termed "the best life in the world."

Life as a player for the Gophers wasn't so bad

either. In his senior year all his basketball skills began to take on a "fine edge" and his performance included 281 rebounds and a 17.4 scoring average. Kevin also led the Gophers into the National Invitation Tournament, which is played in the famed Madison Square Garden in New York City. The team went all the way to the finals before running into the University of Virginia and 7-foot 4-inch Ralph Sampson.

By the time Kevin had put in his final basket for the Gophers he had collected 1,704 points, good enough at the time for second place on the all-time Minnesota scoring list. He also was the team MVP again, earning a spot on the All–Big Ten team for the second year in a row. His growing list of accomplishments included being voted the "outstanding player" of the 1979–80 Aloha Classic held in Hawaii, the MVP at the Pillsbury Classic (three out of four years), and being named first team All-American by United Press International.

Kevin's performance did not escape the attention of the pro-scouts. But before he would be drafted, an interesting thing was taking place in the offices of Red Auerbach, the general manager and president of the Boston Celtics. Auerbach, who led the Celtics to eight straight NBA championships as a coach, is also regarded as the top talent scout in the business. To get the rights to Kevin, he cleverly traded away his two 1980 first-round draft choices (he had picked up a first-round choice in a previous trade) to the Golden State Warriors for center Robert Parish and Golden State's single first-round draft choice.

Auerbach stepped in and used the pick to select the lanky kid from Minnesota, Kevin McHale!

Suddenly, the boy who wanted to play hockey was now on the most famous pro basketball team in the country. Of course, when the mob of reporters surrounded Kevin asking what he thought of being taken by Boston, he gave the press their first taste of his humor and openness: "Where else would a six-ten, white, Irish Catholic kid want to play?"

Boston is where many of the first Irish immigrants settled. It would also be the place where Kevin would get a chance to earn some championship rings. There was one surprise, though. Kevin would not start for Boston. They had another, more important, role in mind.

3

"Let Him Eat Spaghetti!"

Before Kevin McHale could suit up in a Boston uniform, he first had to complete the formalities of signing a contract with the Celtics. That wasn't as easy as it sounds. Kevin wasn't happy with what president Red Auerbach was offering. The contract talks went on during the summer of 1980 with Kevin represented by his agent, John Sandquist, a lawyer from the state of Washington.

Uncertain whether he would come to terms in time for the start of the season, Kevin decided to protect himself from being "left out in the cold" by considering a chance to play pro ball in Italy. When the story hit the press, Celtic coach Bill Fitch responded, "Let him eat spaghetti."

Fortunately, it never came to that. McHale finally signed a three-year contract for an estimated one million dollars. To add to his income, he also signed an endorsement deal with Converse Shoes. Considering the size of McHale's Boston contract, it made sense to think that the Celtics would try to get their money's worth by getting as much playing time out of Kevin as possible. But when the season started, Kevin was not on the floor, but the bench! The Celtics, it seemed, had other plans for the new rookie: instead of starting, McHale would become the team's all-important sixth man. It was a concept started by Auerbach when he coached the team in the 1950s: a player with "starter potential" was put on the bench so he could come in and fire up the team at just the right time. A fresh, first-string-quality player coming in when the opposition is tiring can have enormous impact.

This role fit Kevin like a snug glove. He was the biggest sixth man the Celtics had ever had and when he entered the game, usually late in the first quarter, he was teamed with 6-foot 9½ inch forward Larry Bird and 7-foot ½ inch center Robert Parish. To say the least, it was a devastating front line! His play was so spectacular—especially his defense—that the press began to speculate on using Kevin as a starter. But Boston coach Fitch didn't agree: "He's too valuable as he is. He can do a very difficult thing, which is to go effectively from a dead start into a game that's already in motion."

For Kevin, who was talented enough to start for most NBA teams, it was not a role he minded playing. When asked about it, his comment was "To tell the truth, I kind of like being on the bench. I've had my taste of starting, and I don't need it. I don't consider myself any less efficient a player because I don't start."

Kevin, of course, did not sit idly on the bench. He would keep himself and the others loose by telling jokes and exchanging wisecracks. Then, when he was called into the game, he would reel off his almost unblockable, fade-away jumper. What made the shot almost unstoppable—as the league was beginning to learn—were his long arms, which would normally belong to a man who was seven four!

Kevin's performance was good enough for him to win the league's Rookie of the Year Award. The previous year's winner had also been a Celtic—Larry Bird.

While McHale and the Celtics got ready for the "second" NBA season—the play-offs—the team didn't stop playing practical jokes on one another and the reporters who followed them on the road. They would frustrate the press by temporarily stealing their garment bags. At the airport, the Celtics would do things like page celebrities over the loudspeakers. The favorite of these false announcements was made by Cedric Maxwell, the forward for whom Kevin most often substituted. Maxwell would always page "Dolph Schayes." Schayes is a former All Star who is in the Hall of Fame. He was also the head of the league referees. The joke continued until one day when Dolph actually answered the page!

In the previous year's play-offs, the Celtics had been eliminated by the Philadelphia 76ers 4–1 in the Eastern Conference finals. To win the title they knew that they would have to find a way to stop Julius Erving and Co. It was a tough task, considering that the 76ers had beat the Celtics nine straight times in the Spectrum, Philly's home court. But while the 76ers were having a hard time overcoming the Milwaukee Bucks, Boston was sweeping the Chicago Bulls, 4–0. Philadelphia finally put the Bucks away in the seventh game at the Spectrum, 99–98, and was ready to take on the Celtics to see who would go to the finals.

To the disappointment of all the hopeful Boston fans who filled the famous Boston Garden to see game one, the final score had the 76ers on top, 105–104. The Celtics evened things in the next game, but then had to go on to the Spectrum for the third and fourth game. As usual, the Celtics lost both games and were facing elimination. Back in Boston, the Celtics pulled out a 111–109 victory. Game six went back to Philadelphia. After the Celtics stole the game (100–98), everyone seemed surprised. Everyone, that is, except McHale. With his usual sharp wit he told the press, "Everybody's been talking about the jinx. What about the law of averages? Put chimps on roller skates, let them play in the Spectrum enough times, and sooner or later they'll win."

That victory tied the series and the last game went back to the Boston Garden, where the Celtics won by the narrowest of margins, 91–90. They would not be playing for the championship against the Houston Rockets. Houston was led by Moses Malone, the All-Star center—now with the 76ers—who just happened to upset the championship Lakers in the opening round of the Western Conference play-offs. With Bird and McHale leading the Celtics, the team jumped out to a 3–0 lead. The Rockets recovered to take the next two games, but in the sixth game in Houston the Celtics posted a 102–91 victory.

As the champagne was opened and the celebration started in the clubhouse, everyone was toasting the first Boston championship since the 1975–76 season. McHale couldn't pass up the opportunity to remind Auerbach about the earlier contract hassles: "Thanks, Red, for not letting me play in Italy."

When the team returned to Boston, a crowd of happy fans were on hand, among them Senator Ted Kennedy. His reply to the press on the Celtics 13th championship—the most by any NBA team—was "Basketball was invented in Massachusetts. Now, in 1981, it appears to have a patent on it." The inventor Senator Kennedy was referring to was Dr. James Naismith, who first tried out his idea of basketball in Springfield, Massachusetts, in 1891.

4

"Thank Heaven for Kevin"

Although Kevin was fortunate enough to be on a championship team his first year in the league, it wasn't all peaches and cream. His open, carefree style was in direct contrast to coach Bill Fitch's conservative philosophy. The Celtic coach ran the team with an approach that was labeled a "dictatorship." As one of those close to the scene said, "Kevin has an irreverent bent that can be refreshing. He simply wasn't going to become one of Bill's robots."

If the coach told the players, "the bus leaves at 9:32," Kevin would show up promptly at 9:33. "Go left," the coach said; McHale would go right. And when the coach barred all out-of-town reporters from the team's practice for fear of having his plays stolen, Kevin told a Philadelphia columnist who was waiting in an ice-cold lobby outside the team's practice, "Yeah, we've only been running the same play for fifteen years."

In one incident in the Summit in Houston, Fitch had sent assistant coach Jimmy Rodgers to the top of the stands to check out someone the coach thought was a spy. When it was learned that the person was a maintenance man sneaking a break, Kevin couldn't stop laughing.

When Kevin was asked about the friction between himself and Fitch, he said "Bill's a great coach. We won a championship with him. But after a 30-point loss, he'd show us a tape with nothing but the "low-lights," and twelve guys would be sinking down in their seats. Watching too much tape is like watching too much TV. It may be the Billy Martin [the ex–New York Yankee's manager] syndrome. You get a coach who's a winner, but very volatile, and after a while somebody on the team is going to get burned out. Either you've got to get new players or get a new boss."

It was this controversy that the Celtics carried into the 1981–82 play-offs. After finishing the year with a strong 63–19 record, good enough for first place in the Atlantic Division, the Celtics ran into the fired-up 76ers in the eastern finals and became the victims of Philly's revenge. A year earlier Boston had won the title by ousting the 76ers in their own home court and now Philly returned the favor by winning the seventh game in Boston, 120–106! The one bright note was that during the play-offs Kevin celebrated the birth of his daughter, Kristyn.

If the season ended on a sour note, it got only more bitter when 1982–83 rolled around. The Celtics, with a 56–26 record, finished second in the division to the 76ers. They took on Atlanta in a three-game series and won 2–1, but not without a scuffle between Hawks center Tree Rollins and Celtics guard Danny Ainge. McHale, who is Ainge's closest friend on the team, also got involved. Talking to reporters about the fight, he added a "McHale humor," saying, "I didn't want to see

Danny get hurt. He may be a wimp, but he's also my friend."

The Celtics then took on Milwaukee in the Eastern Conference semifinals. To the shock of everyone, Boston was embarrassed by being blown out by the Bucks four games to zip! For Boston, the team with the proudest tradition in the NBA, it was a great blow. To add to the problems, the Boston owner sold the team.

Nor was team morale helped when in June 1983, the Celtics traded backup center Rick Robey to Phoenix for Dennis Johnson. Although it was a good trade for basketball reasons, Robey was a close friend of both Kevin and Bird. As the Celtics' legendary radio broadcaster, Johnny Most, said, "Bird and Robey were like brothers, and McHale and Robey were "Thumper and Bumper."

But nothing fanned the fire like the news that Kevin's agent, John Sandquist, was shopping around for a new team! McHale was coming to the end of his original contract and could sell his talents to the highest bidder. When the *Boston Globe* found out that Sandquist was talking to the New York Knicks, they ran a cartoon that showed Kevin as a pig wallowing in money. The caption read: The Real McHale."

A great many Celtic fans blamed the team's poor showing on Kevin's contract dispute. It was enough to cause him to say later on that "last year was a sobering experience. The whole thing with the contract and fatherhood forced me to grow up a lot. Life isn't all fun and games. And the media can put a lot of pressure on you." But for Kevin, who hung in despite all the criticism and the problems in the front office, the new 1983–84 season would prove an unforgettable one.

To begin, Fitch resigned from the team to coach the Houston Rockets, and K. C. Jones, a former coach of the Washington Caps, took over the team. Jones had formerly been a star player for the Celtics from 1958 to 1967, and was very familiar with the Boston operation. His style—quiet and supportive—was very different from Fitch's and the team began to return to form. Kevin also had a new contract and was still a Celtic! It was a deal that put him in the millionaire's circle with a four-year, four-million-dollar figure. McHale, who had good reasons for holding out for the money, thought, nonetheless, that there was too much fuss over the negotiations. As he says, "The money thing was blown way out of proportion. I didn't do anything differently because of it. I'm happy about the contract, mainly for my family's security. Beyond that, it doesn't mean much." He even understood the reporters writing what they thought was right: "The press has a job to do and I've got nothing to cover up. If a reporter asks me a question, I'll tell him what I think. Besides, I also think writing is a great art and I like to help people in their art...I do some writing myself, just thoughts I jot down on paper, and then I throw them away. But I really respect people who can write."

With the friction eased, Kevin began to play the kind of basketball that started to get the fans back on his side. Suddenly, the boos turned to cheers, and "finger pointing" turned to praise.

The first evidence of the renewed McHale–Boston love affair came when banners saying THANK HEAVEN FOR KEVIN appeared in the Boston Garden. Of course, when Kevin was asked to explain why he was playing so much better, he couldn't resist throwing in some humor: "Maybe it was something I did during the off-season. But I doubt golfing helps your field-goal percentage. I just have the feeling that every shot I take is going in."

Of course, not every shot went in, but enough apparently, since along with Larry Bird, who was voted the league's MVP, the Celtics came back to take the Atlantic Division with a 62–20 mark. For Kevin's overall great performance he was given the coveted NBA's Sixth Man Award. Kevin also played in his first All-Star game and scored 10 points in 11 minutes. He also played in every game, his forth straight year without missing a game. And while he and his wife, Lynn, who lived during the season in the Boston suburb of Brookline, Massachusetts, were increasing the size of the family with the birth of Michael in December of 1984, Kevin was beginning to get attention from around the league. When Detroit's coach Chuck Daly was asked about Kevin's "sudden" rise to All-Star status, he said, "He's been there all along. McHale just emerged this year."

Detroit's All-Star Kelly Tripucka had a unique opinion of Kevin's talents, "He's not really an athlete. He just does some things really well, like rebound and make the four-foot jump hook. But we sure could use him."

K. C. Jones could only be thankful for having

McHale on the team, especially in the important sixth-man role he plays: "Everybody's not that lucky. I'm very lucky to have that kind of personnel. A guy his size who gives you instant offense, plus blocked shots, gives you an added feel of confidence... the important people are the sixth men. They're really starters. John Havlicek [ex-Celtic and current Hall of Famer] came off the bench. Bobby Jones, McHale... they're going to be right in front of everybody when the game's on the line."

During the play-offs the Celtics marched toward the title by beating Washington, New York, and Milwaukee. All that remained were the tough Lakers, led by Magic Johnson and Kareem Abdul-Jabbar. The Lakers took the first game at Boston before the Celtics came back to tie the series. But after Boston was routed 137–104 in L.A., Kevin pulled off a play that seemed to ignite the Celtics when he lassoed 6-foot, 8-inch Kurt Rambis around the neck in trying to stop a Laker score. Of course both benches emptied, and the Celtics won in overtime, 129–125. Although it provided the necessary fuel for the fire, it was not a popular move—at least not in L.A. That was something that Kevin discovered when he took Lynn and the kids to Disneyland and was booed by Mickey Mouse!

With the series tied, the next game went back to Boston. The Celtics won but found themselves even again after losing the sixth game in L.A. But with the seventh game in Boston, Bird, Kevin, and the other Celtics proved the better, if not stronger, team with a 111–102 victory. McHale now had his second championship ring and Boston their fifteenth league title. In the celebration that followed, McHale provided the most colorful description of the Laker–Celtic clash: "It was a case of the Teamsters, the hard hats, and the miners [Boston] taking on the M.D.'s [L.A.] in their Mercedes, the lawyers in their three-piece suits, and the movie stars of Hollywood, and winning by getting their hands dirty."

Be it a basket, a blocked shot, or a wisecrack, Boston fans could count to seven and say, "Thank Heaven for Kevin!"

5

Kevin McHale: "The Ultimate Luxury"

Kevin McHale was now regarded as the best "sixth man" in basketball. He could come off the bench and because of his height help create severe match ups for the opposition, such as the game against Detroit where he scored 19 of his 29 points in the fourth quarter. Most of the scoring came off of 6-foot 8-inch Cliff Levingston. It was a situation which McHale colorfully labeled "the torture chamber."

K. C. Jones, the Boston coach, was well aware of what Kevin could do in a game: "From a coach's viewpoint, Kevin is the ultimate luxury. I can use him at center or either forward spot. He can give me scoring or help us protect a lead with his defense. With him coming off the bench, my options up front are almost unlimited."

When forward Cedric Maxwell got hurt toward the middle of the 1984–85 season, some of Jones's options became limited and he changed McHale from a Super Sub to a Super Starter. So what does McHale do playing almost the whole game? Simple: he sets a Celtic single-game scoring record with a whopping 56 points, breaking the previous record of 53 points held by Larry Bird!

The game came against the Detroit Pistons on March 3, 1985. Kevin, of course, would not take full credit for the record. As he said, "Larry would get the rebounds and just give me the ball to lay it in. It was Bird's ability. I was just renting it for a while." In fact, Kevin didn't even mind giving up the record when Bird poured in 60 points against Atlanta on March 12.

As the team rolled to another Atlantic Division title with a 63–19 record, Kevin was still making the reporters laugh. Asked about his reputation for being smart, he said, "Gee, I haven't had a deep thought since my history exam at the University of Minnesota." McHale, of course, can get a little more serious about the subject: "Well, yeah, I read—biographies, fiction, nonfiction, all kinds of things. But it's not all intellectual stuff. I read a lot of popular fiction."

Kevin's observations on living in the East also caused a few chuckles, such as when he said, "It's different here. Back home, if you see a car in a snowdrift you just walk over and start pushing the car. Here, you see a guy stuck and everybody says, 'Good, that's one less guy I'll have to worry about today.'"

When the Celtics entered the play-offs, they reached the finals by beating Cleveland, Detroit and Philadelphia. But when they took on the Lakers again in the finals, the team became part of a jinx that has haunted every NBA champion since 1969. That was the last time any team won back-to-back titles. Back then it happened to be the Celtics who turned the trick. Even Kevin's series-leading 26-point average couldn't keep a determined Laker team away from the title as the Celtics bowed out in 6 games.

Most surprising about losing the last game was that it took place in Boston, where Kevin scored 32 points but fouled out with 5 minutes 32 seconds left. The Celtics had never been eliminated in a final series at home. Kevin and the other Celtics were in a state of disbelief over the 111–100 loss. Even so, it didn't take away the joy of playing in Boston. As Kevin says, "There's still no place I'd rather be than the Garden."

Even though the season was a disappointment, both McHale and Bird were able to have some satisfaction by again winning individual honors. Bird became the league MVP again and Kevin captured his second straight "Sixth Man Award."

What McHale didn't know was that come the next season he would no longer be in the running for the award. Forward Cedrick Maxwell would be wearing the uniform of the Los Angeles Clippers and the Portland Trail Blazers' Bill Walton was now wearing a Celtic Jersey. Walton was made the team's "sixth man" and Kevin remained a starter.

And the results? Boston won an incredible 67 games—the fourth best ever in the NBA! It included a 50–1 Boston Garden record that saw the Celtics win 41 straight at home. Kevin, who starred at both ends of the court, was a workhorse for the team, and once again was selected for the NBA All-Star Game.

But for Kevin, who spends all his time with his family when he's home and sees friends from high school whenever he's in Milwaukee (leaving space for them on his hotel room floor), the only thing that was really important this season in terms of basketball was taking the championship back from the Lakers.

But to everyone's surprise, the Lakers never even reached the finals since they were eliminated by the upstart Houston Rockets, who were led by 7-foot 4-inch Ralph Sampson and 7-foot Akeem "the Dream" Olajuwon, also known as Houston's "Twin Towers." In the meantime the Celtics swept past the Chicago Bulls in spite of Michael Jordan's one-game play-off record of 63 points, beat Atlanta in five games, and eliminated Milwaukee in four straight games to reach the finals. The only roadblock that remained was the Rockets, who were coached by Bill Fitch, the former Celtics coach.

Boston won the first two games before Houston stunned the Celtics by coming back from 8 points behind with only 4 minutes left. In game four the Celtics were barely able to overcome the Rockets as a result of McHale's game high 33 points and a Walton score on a rebound with a minute and a half left. Going into the next game with a 3–1 edge caused Kevin to say, "We want it to end here."

But Houston would not quit and when Sampson was ejected from the game because of a fight with the Celtics 6-foot 2-inch Jerry Sichting, the Rockets ignited and won 111–96. That game was in Houston. When the series moved back to the Boston Garden with its close quarters, the Celtics fans wouldn't let up on Sampson or the other Rockets. Neither would the Celtics, who won easily, 114–97. For McHale and Bird, who did all the scoring in a 13–2 streak when Boston was on top, 22–21 in the first quarter, it was an easy victory. Both forwards got 29 points each as Boston led by as many as 30 points.

Boston now had its sixteenth championship. And as Kevin was tasting the victory champagne for the third time in six years, he was providing the reporters with good newspaper copy. The media was also supplying good copy about Kevin. *Sports Illustrated* put him on their cover the week after the clincher, and the *New York Times* did an entire feature entitled "NBA Disorder: Kevinmchaleitis," which dealt mainly with how desperate each of the other teams in the league were to somehow come up with a player to neutralize Kevin McHale and give their own team a chance against the Celtics.

To ward off any further contract problems, the Celtics awarded Kevin with a new contract—starting in the 1987–88 season—for $4.4 million over four years, with an additional $1.6 million option for a fifth year.

For Kevin, who gets involved with children and contributing to charities, and doesn't really voice his opinion on political issues, there is one subject that he is vocal about: "Acid rain. I'm very concerned about the environment. I like to fish and hunt, I like the wilderness, and I guess if I were going to stand up for something publicly, it would be the protection of the environment."

When Kevin is asked about the future, he is quick to say that he intends calling it quits around 1990. The reason he gives is "I'm too family oriented. I'll go back to school, and then maybe I'll try real life." Or, as he adds with a smile, "Then again, maybe I'll become a professional backgammon player. I used to be pretty good at that."

There are probably a couple of other things that Kevin is good at, like winning championships and cutting a swift path to Basketball's Hall of Fame. Even though he jests about how he might just end up as a "question in somebody's Trivial Pursuit game," the consensus is that his performance and humor will be remembered long after he shoots his last basket.

McHale leans around the Pistons' Kelly Tripucka to pass off to Larry Bird.
(AP/Wide World Photos)

Then goes downcourt and stuffs Isiah Thomas.
(AP/Wide World Photos)

Ouch! It's rough out there!
(UPI/Bettmann Newsphotos)

And it gets worse!
(AP/Wide World Photos)

Kevin battles Magic Johnson in a 1985 play-off game...
(AP/Wide World Photos)

But Celtics lose the game and the play-offs.
(AP/Wide World Photos)

Kevin bounces back with a stuff against Akeem "The Dream" in the last game of the 1986 play-offs...
(AP/Wide World Photos)

Which produces the sweet smile of victory.
(AP/Wide World Photos)

"Air" Jordan goes over Magic Johnson while leading the 1984 Olympic team to a victory over the NBA All-Stars.
(AP/Wide World Photos)

Michael won the Eastman Award for being named the top player in college basketball.
(AP/Wide World Photos)

Then he won the NBA Rookie-of-the-Year Award.
(AP/Wide World Photos)

Back to the games with a hook over Akeem.
(AP/Wide World Photos)

"Air" Jordan's flight is canceled by an injury in 1985.
(AP/Wide World Photos)

Up, up, and away...
(UPI/Bettmann Newsphotos)

Michael soars over Kevin McHale.
(AP/Wide World Photos)

Two points during a record-setting scoring performance in the 1986 play-offs against the Celtics.
(AP/Wide World Photos)

MICHAEL JORDAN

1
Flying High

"Slim, trim and cat quick" is the way Michael Jordan describes himself. As anyone who's seen him play knows, he is all those things and much more. As a star of the Chicago Bulls in the National Basketball Association, he has, in two short pro seasons, caused people to search for new superlatives.

His style of play, which is "originality in motion," includes an arsenal of weapons that leaves the opposition shaking their heads. Michael Jordan doesn't simply play basketball. He creates a special world that allows him to do things like fly and hang suspended in the air. Of course, it only seems that Jordan can defy the laws of gravity. In reality, he is levelheaded enough to have both feet planted firmly on the ground.

But not when he plays basketball!

Then he is a high-flying aerialist who brings the crowds to their feet with one of his double-pump, awesome jump shots. And when he is not flying—for points or rebounds—he is stealing the ball. And when he is not scoring on the inside, he is swishing the net from 20 feet out. It is such a dazzling performance, that reporters around the country have described Michael Jordan as "poetry in motion" or an "eagle in flight" who performs "aerial artistry." As Julius Erving, basketball's most famous pre-Jordan aerialist said when asked about Jordan, "Certainly he has a very charismatic style to excite people. He flies. He handles the ball. He makes steals. He gambles on defense. He does all the things you need to do to break a game open."

Before Michael Jordan started flying in the pros, he was flying away with a national basketball championship for North Carolina College, an Olympic gold medal for the United States, and a long list of other awards. But what separates him even more is the same grace and poise that he exhibits off the court. He is always ready to sign an autograph, give an interview, and have a warm hello for anyone he meets. His easygoing and open personality was best summed up by his mother when she said, "Michael really never meets a stranger."

The many thousands of fans and hundreds of reporters whom he has met would certainly all agree with Michael's mom. So would his teammates, opponents, coaches, or anyone whom Jordan has had contact with in his twenty-three years. Michael is so popular that the Nike Shoe company brought out a line of basketball shoes and sporting goods named Air Jordan.

2
The Giant of the Family

Air Jordan first floated into the world on February 17, 1963, in Brooklyn, New York. Officially named Michael Jeffery Jordan by his parents, James and Delores, he was the third child of a solid middle-class family that was eventually to include five children. Oddly enough, Michael, who eventually hit 6 feet 6 inches, was the only member of the family to pass the 6-foot mark. It probably was the reason that Michael Jordan is in the National Basketball Association today, rather than on a major league baseball diamond. He is that kind of super athlete.

As things turned out, Michael Jordan would not find his fame in Brooklyn. James Jordan resettled the family in Wilmington, North Carolina, and Michael, along with his brothers, Larry and James, and his sisters, Roslyn and Delores, all enjoyed the comfort and security of a tight-knit family that shared a common philosophy. If there was one motto in the Jordan household it was WORK. As Michael's father, who holds a supervisory position at General Electric in Wilmington, said, "The way it is in our family is that we try to make something happen rather than waiting around for it to happen. We believe the surest way is to work toward making it the way you want it."

It just might be one of the reasons why Michael Jordan is now considered one of the most exciting basketball players in the world today. But basketball, oddly enough, was not the first sport that Michael took up, nor his favorite. His first love was baseball. But whatever he cared to play—baseball, football, basketball, track and field—he was always fortunate enough to have the encouragement and complete support of his parents. They attended almost every game Michael played, including his college games.

His mother, who heads a customer relations department for a bank, is given credit by Michael's father for supplying the "winning edge." As James Jordan says, "Michael got his competitive nature from his mother. She's a winner."

But if Michael's mother gave him the winning spirit, it was his father who gave him his special "tongue-wagging" trademark. His father's habit of pushing out his tongue whenever he's washing the car in the family backyard is a trait that Michael displays whenever he's burning up the opposition on the basketball court.

But Michael Jordan wasn't always burning up the opposition in basketball. Before he could become the player he is today, he had to follow his father's work ethic on a strict and daily routine. He was also faced with the fact that he was physically a late bloomer and did not reach six feet in height until he entered Laney High School in Wilmington, North Carolina.

The idea to pursue basketball came from his mother. Michael had suffered a couple of injuries while playing football and she urged him to try a "less dangerous sport." He was fourteen at the time, and up to that point had never really taken the game of basketball seriously.

Aside from that, he was still developing, still trying to catch up to his height, which went up four inches between his sophomore and junior year. It made him slow and weak and almost caused him to miss making the varsity in his junior year. But then, with his hours of constant practice and dogged determination to improve, he started to develop quickly.

One of the things he did was to work on his game day after day, playing with his brother Larry on the regulation basketball court that their father had built in the backyard of their home. Larry, who was the oldest, was no slouch. In fact, if it weren't for Larry's height, he might have gone on to join Michael in college and the pros. According to Michael, Larry is just as gifted in basketball. When Michael talks about their days in the backyard, he has nothing but praise for his brother: "Larry always used to beat me on the backyard court. His vertical jump is higher than mine. He's got the dunks and some 360s and most all the same stuff I got. And he's five-seven! He's my inspiration!"

It was an inspiration that carried over into Laney High. They both played basketball there and led the team from the backcourt positions. It was a great experience that Michael will always remember. It is the reason why he selected Number 23 for his jersey uniform. With typical Michael Jordan originality, he simply cut his brother's Number 45 in half, or at least as close as he could come without having to wear a ½ on his uniform.

While in high school, Michael not only played basketball but starred in football and baseball as well. He was even on the track team, where he was considered above average as a long and high jumper. In football he quarterbacked the team, and on the baseball diamond he pitched, and played shortstop and the outfield. But it was in basketball that he excelled to the point where, in his senior year, he was named to most prep All-American teams.

By the end of Michael's high school career there was no doubt that his was a very special talent. He could have had a full scholarship to almost any basketball school in the country, but he wound up selecting the University of North Carolina for a very special reason. And it wasn't because North Carolina was considered the basketball temple of the East and the dream of almost every high school basketball player in the country. Michael, in fact, never had any special feeling for the Tar Heels. As he says, "Growing up, I hated North Carolina. I was a [North Carolina] State fan; David Thompson was the man. My mom liked Phil Ford, but I couldn't stand him or any of them Carolina guys. I rooted for Marquette in the '77 championship game. My mom got mad." All that was true until after Michael got a chance to visit the Tar Heel campus in Chapel Hill. As Michael says, "The coaches didn't even know I was there. I saw the place as a student, not as a recruit." It was enough to convince Michael that UNC was his choice.

Michael also discovered a great friend at Chapel

Hill. In the summer before starting classes as a freshman he met Buzz Peterson at Dean Smith's summer basketball camp. Smith is the head coach at North Carolina. Buzz was also going to play basketball for the Tar Heels in the fall and so he and Michael had a lot in common. But as Buzz now tells the story, something that he and Michael now laugh about, it was Michael who had most of the butterflies that day: "This is my first camp," Michael said, "and I'm scared."

What made their friendship—and especially the friendship between their parents—so special was that the Jordans were black and the Petersons white. That might not be so unusual in many parts of the country, but in the South it was unusual; especially unusual was the way in which the parents shared their talented sons. As Michael's dad says, "It's a beautiful friendship. From the first time we met Buzz's parents, at the camps, we hit it off. They're likable and easy to know. We've always looked on Michael's friends as our sons, and we advise them as we do Michael."

In addition to starting college with a new friend, Michael also got another surprise. His sister, Roslyn, who was a year younger, had skipped her last year at Laney High and was going to join Michael at North Carolina. All that support made it easier to take on the challenge of college and big-time school basketball. But there was still the question of how well Michael would do against tougher competition.

Would he be just another "good" college player, or would he dominate?

It wasn't long before the answer came.

3
Blue Heaven

Even before Michael Jordan got to the University of North Carolina to play for head coach Dean Smith, he knew it was a great honor to be wearing the powder blue uniform of the Tar Heels. One of the things that made the basketball program at North Carolina so special was the system that Coach Smith has operated under in his twenty-four years (going through the 1985–86 season) as head coach: the seniors on the team make the rules; he enforces them! That means that the freshmen on the team, no matter how talented, draw dog duties. Even though Michael was able to break into the starting lineup on an excellent team that included James Worthy (now with the Lakers) and Sam Perkins (now with Dallas), he and the other freshmen had to help the team managers at home and on the road in addition to chasing loose balls in practice.

Michael really didn't mind following all the rules. After all, he was the only freshman starter on a team that lost the national championship to coach Bobby Knight and Indiana in the previous year's (1980–81) NCAA finals. He was happy to make any contribution to the team, as was Buzz Peterson, who went to the bench to become the team's all-important sixth man before being sidelined by a knee injury in midseason 1982-83.

In addition to following all the team rules, Buzz and Michael also made a rule of their own: they both decided to limit their social activities until the season was over. So in between classes, studying, and basketball, they either played pool, which is Michael's game, or golf, which is Buzz's game. They also shared a Monopoly board, which Jordan attacked with the same determination he applies to everything else. Also, to cut down on expenses, they shared each other's clothes, even though Michael is a few inches taller than Buzz.

As the Tar Heels started on their drive for what they hoped would be a national title, Jordan's great floor play helped lead the team to a championship in the tough Atlantic Coast Conference. His 13.5 average points a game and his 149 rebounds from his guard-forward position were enough to help give UNC a regular season record of 32-2 and have him voted the ACC Rookie of the Year. Now all they had ahead of them were the likes of Patrick Ewing of Georgetown, a seven-foot-plus center who could easily dominate the game. It was not going to be an easy task.

When Michael and the other Tar Heels arrived in New Orleans for the NCAA finals after having beaten Villanova, 70-60 in the East finals, all eyes were on Worthy and Ewing. Jordan, it seemed, was not well known outside of his own conference. Then, as UNC beat Houston 68-63 and Georgetown got by Louisville by a 50-46 score, it was showdown time!

The game went back and forth with Georgetown taking a 62–61 lead with the time running out. But then Worthy, who was the game's MVP, got a pass to Jordan with 15 seconds left. He climbed a few steps of his "air ladder" and got off a 17-foot jumper that found the basket and gave the Tar Heels a 63–62 victory and the 1982 national title! Jordan became an instant hero to the millions of TV viewers watching the game.

Coach Smith, overjoyed and floating on cloud nine, like the rest of the North Carolina team, could not give Jordan enough praise: "I've seen other great athletes, but Michael has the intelligence, the court savvy, and then you add the burning desire, a dedication. And add to that a charisma. He was a hero so many times at the end of games—it was uncanny. It really was."

As Jordan took home his championship ring and the honor of being named to All-Tournament teams in the NCAA final four and the ACC championships, he suddenly found himself bathed in the national spotlight. So dramatic was his game-winning jumper that the telephone company in Chapel Hill–Carrboro area memorialized the event by putting a picture of the great shot on the cover of the phone directory!

When Michael returned to UNC in the fall to start the 1982–83 season, James Worthy was no longer there. He had chosen to pass up his senior year and enter the NBA. That left the main burden on Jordan and Sam Perkins. And while they turned in excellent seasons, the Tar Heels were unable to repeat their triumph. Jordan led UNC in points scored and steals. Those stats and his overall exciting play won him the honor of being unanimously selected as a consensus All-American and to bring Michael the greatest individual trophy in college basketball: the Sporting News College Player of the Year award! In winning it he beat out 7-foot 4-inch Ralph Sampson. If there was any doubt that Michael Jordan had arrived, that trophy silenced all doubters.

But the year did not end without Jordan and Perkins getting their chance at another championship. That was the 1983 Pan American games held in Caracas, Venezuela. The USA team—with Jordan leading the scoring—took home the gold medal.

When Jordan returned home, he continued to play basketball whenever he could. As a favor to make sure Michael would relax and take it easy, his mother took away his car keys! But she could only keep him "rested" for so long. When he returned to UNC, he turned in another incredible season, leading the Tar Heels to an ACC championship and as far as the East NCAA semifinal round before losing to Bobby Knight and Indiana, 72–68. If you wonder how good Michael's 1982–83 junior season was, just look what happened when it came time for the College Player of the Year award. Jordan was again named best college basketball player in the country!

The talk that was circulating at the time was whether or not Michael would go on to the pros or return to UNC for his last year. He had already accumulated 1,788 points—ninth highest in UNC history—and had a chance to be the all-time leader. Michael did want to return, but with All-American Sam Perkins graduating it meant that his play—which was limited by all the zones, double and triple teaming, and slowdowns of college basketball—would be limited, especially since he was now the "main threat" to stop. Because of all these factors it was thought best that he consider the pro offers. It was a decision that Coach Smith and his parents endorsed.

Jordan, of course, went on to the Chicago Bulls. But his loyalty to UNC, where he has since returned to work toward his degree in geography, is as strong as ever. As Michael Jordan says, "I always wear a pair of North Carolina blue basketball trunks under my Bulls uniform and under my street clothes. I'm not superstitious, but I do consider them to be my lucky charm. They are a piece of Blue Heaven."

But before signing any pro contract, there was one last amateur stop Michael had to make. It was in Los Angeles, home of the 1984 Summer Olympic Games.

4
"Jump, Jump, Jump"

When Michael Jordan got to Los Angeles for the 1984 Olympic Games he had some of the best company in college basketball with him. Led by Indiana head coach Bobby Knight, the team included three towering centers in Patrick Ewing, Joe Kleine, and Jon Koncak; forwards Wayman Tisdale, Sam Perkins, and Jeff Turner; swingmen Jordan, Chris Mullen, and Vern Fleming. The ball handlers were Al Wood and Steve Alford, and defensive pickpocket Alvin Robertson. It wasn't just a good team—it was a great one. With the exception of Alford, now a senior at Indiana, every player has gone on to the pros.

By the time the team, with Jordan as cocaptain, got to the finals, there was little question of how good the Americans were. With the high-flying Jordan leading the attack, the U.S. destroyed Spain 101–68 in the opening round, even though Jordan had to leave the game early in the second half because of a sprained ankle. But he returned and the U.S. beat Canada, France, and West Germany by large margins. One of the scores that proved the most embarrassing was a 120–62 scalding of the French team!

For the gold-medal game, the Americans took on Spain again, and although the Spaniards tried to learn from the first disaster, they could not overcome the great defense or scoring power of the U.S. team. They were so dominated that Jordan left the game early as his teammates rolled up a 32-point final victory margin! Spanish head coach Antonio Diaz-Miguel, who considered Jordan "an easy choice" for best player, was impressed enough with Michael's Magic to say, "He's not human. He's a rubber man." One of coach Diaz-Miguel's players, Fernando Martin, had an even better description of Jordan's game: "Michael Jordan? Jump, jump, jump. Very quick. Very fast. Very, very good. Jump, jump, jump."

As the team celebrated its gold-medal triumph, Coach Knight would not let the victory be spoiled by the Russians' absence. When questioned by reporters he told them, "We'll beat the Russians' butts anywhere they want to play. I've seen them play a lot in the last two years. They can't play defense ... You tell me the Russians can play these guys. There is no way the Russians can come close to this bunch." Many agreed: the team was considered the best in U.S. history, even better than the 1960 Olympic squad led by Hall of Famers Oscar Robertson and Jerry West. Or as Spain's coach said, "Fifty years ahead of everyone else."

Besides adding the brightest of all his trophies to his overcrowded collection, Jordan also used the opportunity to work with Knight—considered one of the best coaches in the country—to improve his already incredible abilities. As he said before leaving Los Angeles, "Coach Knight helped me to concentrate and do things without a lot of lallygagging around." But would Michael have liked to play under the screaming, fiercely competitive, intense Knight for four years? "I'd have to think about that for a while" was his answer.

In the meantime, what Jordan had to think about was the start of his pro career with the Chicago Bulls. To the surprise of many people, Michael was "only" the third selection in the draft. Houston, selecting first, chose Akeem Olajuwon of Houston University; and Portland, with the second pick, took Sam Bowie of Kentucky. Both were seven-footers. Teammate Perkins was taken fourth by Cleveland, before being traded to Dallas. Jordan, of course, understood that after Olajuwon, Bowie was the best big man available.

But Dirk Minniefield, Bowie's close friend who was a late cut by the Bulls for the 1984–85 NBA season, had a different feeling about the draft: "Houston and Portland are both going to be sorry they didn't draft him."

For the fans of Chicago the only thing they were sorry about was that Jordan had not been there sooner. The franchise, which had managed to get to the play-offs only once in the past seven seasons, was badly in need of a supply of excitement.

5

"Here Comes Mr. Jordan!"

With his great show in the Summer Olympics still fresh in the mind of basketball and nonbasketball fans alike, Michael Jordan was expected to set off fireworks in Chicago. He was already being called the "next Julius Erving." And no matter where Jordan and the Bulls went, there were throngs of newspaper, magazine, and TV reporters, and thousands of screaming fans. It was even more than Jordan could believe, especially when it was happening during the exhibition season!

In one game in Gary, Indiana, screaming teenage girls mobbed Jordan, causing such a scene that teammate Orlando Woolridge said, "Michael Jackson, eat your heart out." Jordan could only shake his head and say, "I mean, I haven't even played a regular-season game yet."

That, of course, didn't matter. Not to Kevin Loughery, coach of the Bulls, or the fans of Chicago, who were trying to forget last year's finish when the team had the second worst record in the NBA, and only one game better than the Indiana Pacers!

Teammate Jawann Oldham, watching Jordan perform a series of gravity-defying moves against the Milwaukee Bucks in an early season victory, was moved enough by the performance—which included flying dunks with three and four Bucks on board—to say, "He's God's child. Let God deal with him." In a more astonishing performance, Jordan not only helped bring the Bulls from behind the Clippers in a game in Los Angeles, but did it in such a way that even the home crowd cheered him! First he made an 18-foot jumper that tied the game with 1:26 left. He then stopped Norm Nixon and forced an airball, which center Caldwell Jones grabbed. Jordan, then chasing a long outlet pass from Jones, caught up with the ball at halfcourt. He scooped up the ball and started his climb for a patented Jordan dunk when Derek Smith of the Clippers caught up with him and applied a midair bear hug. Then, with both men heading for the floor, Jordan—barely able to see the basket—got off the shot. Amazingly enough, it went in! A free shot followed and the Bulls went on to win, 104–100. The crowd, stunned by the basket, broke into applause while one fan shouted, "USA, USA," as a reminder of Jordan's play in the Olympics. All Derek Smith could say was, "Incredible. Most people wouldn't have gotten the ball out of their hands."

As Michael continued to burn up the league, giving the Bulls a shot at the play-offs for the first time in three years, he continued to amaze his opponents in the NBA. As Larry Bird of the Celtics said, after seeing him perform close up, "Best. Never seen anyone like him. Phenomenal. One of a kind. He's the best, ever. Yep, at this stage in his career, he's doing more than I ever did. I couldn't do what he did as a rookie. Heck, there was one drive tonight, he had the ball in his right hand, then he took it down, then he brought it back up. I got a hand on it, fouled him, and he still scored. You have to play the game to realize how difficult that is. You see that and figure, 'Well, what the heck can you do?'"

Not much when you consider the 41 points, 12 rebounds, and 7 assists that Bird was talking about.

New York Knicks coach Hubie Brooks had his own compliment for Jordan: "The young man is blessed with so much natural talent, and then he plays at such a fever pitch. Jordan is always—or most nights—playing or performing on all cylinders at the top of his potential. He's a lot like Bird. They are special."

But while Jordan was able to almost double the crowds in Chicago Stadium and make the Bulls the fourth best road team in the NBA, he could not get Chicago over their center problems. The team wound up with a 38–44 record. Not very good, but good enough to take the Bulls to the NBA play-offs and give the fans some hope for the future. Although the team was eliminated in the play-offs by Milwaukee, it took nothing away from Jordan's spectacular season. He was not only selected for the NBA All-Star team, but was named Rookie of the Year, second team All-NBA, and won the Schick Pivotal Player-of-the-Year award. He not only scored more points than Bird, Erving, and Magic Johnson in their rookie seasons, but wound up third in the league scoring average with 28.2, and first in total points with 2,316. His 196 steals were fourth best in the league.

He became only the third player since Dave Cowens and Bird to lead a team in rebounds, assists, steals, and points in the same season.

For Jordan himself, the season was unexpected but welcome: "I really didn't know how good I could be [in the pros]. Everyone on the coaching staff at UNC was telling me I'd do fine, but you really don't know. I went in with a clear head, just to go out and try to contribute and do the best I can. I knew expectations were way above my head. I never thought I could reach them, but I surprised myself and I surprised a lot of them."

Some of the other people who Jordan surprised were not connected with the NBA. At George Washington U., where Michael went to film a commercial for the Special Olympics, he worked with retarded children suffering from Down's syndrome, and made some special friends. One in particular was a girl named Tania Przbyia, who got an instant crush on the NBA's hottest attraction. After Michael helped her make a layup, she hugged him. Then, as he started to leave, Tania bowed her head. Jordan saw the tears rolling down her cheeks and he walked back over, lifted her head, and gave her a big hug.

Michael went on that appearance even though he had only had five hours sleep following a game against the Washington Bullets in which he helped the Bulls clinch the play-off spot. It only proves what his mother says: none of the success has spoiled Michael or changed his "good manners." As far as Michael was concerned, doing something for less fortunate people was only a chance of saying thanks, or, as he expressed it, "Basketball, all my fans, they have given a lot to me. This is my way of giving something back to the community. I'll always remember when I wasn't so popular."

6

Air Jordan Soars!

Aside from burning up the NBA, Michael Jordan was also setting fire to the business world. Along with his agent David Falk, who is a senior vice president at ProServ, a company representing athletes, Michael signed endorsement contracts with several companies. In all, it brought him an estimated $1.7 million over and above his healthy basketball salary. Even Falk was amazed that Michael was such a hot property: "In basketball, that's virtually unheard of. And we've rejected more offers than we've accepted. Nobody, including me, expected him to be that big."

Nike is where Jordan made his richest deal, signing a contract worth an estimated $2.5 million! Nike would introduce a line of gym apparel, flight bags, and basketball shoes, all under the name Air Jordan, and Michael would receive a royalty on every item sold. But, of course, no one knew how well the line would be accepted, especially the three-quarter red-black-and-white leather shoes with the special "air-cushioned soul." At the time Michael said, "Hopefully, little kids will pick up on them."

They did a lot more than that. In nine months time, the Air Jordan shoe and the name itself became so popular that the line grossed $90–$100 million for Nike! Even small toddlers became part of the boom with the introduction of Baby Jordan, which has already sold more than 100,000 pairs.

Although Michael only made commercials for Coca-Cola and McDonald's (where he can often be seen eating), he did get involved with Chevrolet in a promotion campaign that created such excitement that the head of a Chicago Chevrolet dealership was moved to say, "No promotion has ever worked better for me than Michael Jordan. People just keep on coming in and telling my sales people, 'I want the Michael Jordan Blazer.'" The Blazer is a Chevy pickup truck that Michael drives, along with his silver Corvette.

Michael's popularity wasn't limited to the States. In the summer of 1984 he went to Europe on the Jordan Tour and wowed them in Italy, France, and England. And everywhere that he went, thousands came to see him. Of course, Jordan didn't return home before appearing at a "Save the Children" fashion show in London. Michael also did a little more than just demonstrate how well he can model clothes. He gave a donation on his behalf and on behalf of Princess Anne, Queen Elizabeth's daughter.

But the upcoming 1985–86 season would bring a dark cloud and temporarily wipe the smile from Michael's face as a severe injury would sideline him for much of the season and test his determination to overcome obstacles.

7

A Record-Setting Performance!

In a game against the Golden State Warriors on October 29, in California, Jordan hit the floor during one of his high-flying plays and injured his ankle. It was only the third game of the season. But a few days later it was discovered that the mishap was much more than a sprain. Jordan had cracked a bone in his left foot! For the fans, players, and new head coach Stan Albeck, who had come over from the Nets, it was a disaster: Jordan would not return until next season!

But the fact didn't stop the fans around the league from making Michael the top vote getter on the East squad for the NBA All-Star game! Of course, Michael couldn't play, but it showed just how much he was appreciated by the fans. What the fans didn't know was that Jordan had a surprise in store. He would return to the Bulls starting lineup for the last few weeks of the season and lead them into the play-offs!

It was a move that even the Chicago management was against. They didn't want him to come back too soon and risk greater injury. But there was no stopping Michael.

It would take the Celtics, whom the Bullets had drawn in the first round of the play-offs, to end Michael and the Bulls' season. In the first game

Michael scored 49 points in a 123–104 losing effort. He then almost single-handedly evened the series with an incredible 63-point outburst! It forced the game into overtime—not once, but twice. But when the final buzzer sounded, the Celtics had the game, 135–131. For Michael, the one consolation was that the 63 points broke the NBA all-time play-off scoring record set by the Lakers' great Elgin Baylor back in 1962. In the third game the Celtics, in awe of Jordan's performance, double-teamed him to hold him to 18 points in eliminating the Bulls, 122–104. Michael's three-game total of 131 points in a three-game series wiped out the 1960 mark of 116 set by the legendary Wilt Chamberlain. A very impressed Bird said, "Maybe the guy is God disguised as Michael Jordan."

Michael's play commands respect throughout the league. The Detroit Pistons' Isiah Thomas had this to say: "He'll probably be one of the guys who invents a new position."

All Jim Thomas of the Indiana Packers could talk about was Jordan's surprising quickness: "I don't know if his first step is legal because I've never had time to judge it." And the Phoenix Suns' Michael Holton, after trying to guard Jordan, could only say, "All I saw were the bottoms of his shoes." Yet it was teammate Sidney Green who summed up what every player must feel when they come up against Jordan's speed and deft moves: "He's the truth, the whole truth, and nothing but the truth."

For Michael, there are still a lot of goals to accomplish. In thinking about his career so far and what the future might hold, he said, "I hope I can say I did my best, achieved a lot, and won a couple of world championships."

It's obvious that his determination and talent will allow him to achieve his first two goals, and if Chicago can come up with a few key players, Michael might also achieve the World Championships. Watching him perform one of his unique "aerial ballets" makes you think Michael "Air" Jordan can do anything he wants with a basketball.

KEVIN McHALE
University of Minnesota Record

Year	G.	Min.	FGA	FGM	Pct.	FTA	FTM	Pct.	Reb.	Pts.	Avg.
76-77	27	....	241	133	.552	77	58	.753	218	324	12.0
77-78	26	....	242	143	.591	77	54	.701	192	340	13.1
78-79	27	....	391	202	.517	96	79	.823	259	483	17.9
79-80	32	....	416	236	.567	107	85	.794	281	557	17.4
Totals	112	....	1290	714	.553	357	276	.773	950	1704	15.2

NBA Regular Season Record

Season–Team	G.	Min.	FGA	FGM	Pct.	FTA	FTM	Pct.	Ast.	PF	Dq.	Stl.	Blk.	Pts.	Avg.
80-81–Boston	82	1645	666	355	.533	159	108	.679	55	260	3	27	151	818	10.0
81-82–Boston	82	2332	875	465	.531	248	187	.754	91	264	1	30	185	1117	13.6
82-83–Boston	82	2345	893	483	.541	269	193	.717	104	241	3	34	192	1159	14.1
83-84–Boston	82	2577	1055	587	.556	439	336	.765	104	243	5	23	126	1511	18.4
84-85–Boston	79	2653	1062	605	.570	467	355	.760	141	234	3	28	120	1565	19.8
85-86–Boston	68	2397	978	561	.574	420	326	.776	181	192	2	29	134	1448	21.3
Totals	475	13,949	5,529	3,056	.553	2002	1505	.752	676	1434	17	171	908	7,618	16.0

Three-Point Field Goals: 1980–81, 0-for-2. 1982–83, 0-for-1. 1983–84, 1-for-3 (.333). 1984–85, 0-for-6. 1985–86, No Attempts.
Totals: 1-for-12 (.083)

NBA Play-off Stats

	G.	Min.	FGA	FGM	Pct.	FTA	FTM	Pct.	Ast.	PF	Dq.	Stl.	Blk.	Pts.	Avg
1980-81–Boston	17	296	113	61	.540	36	23	.693	14	51	1	4	25	145	8.5
1981-82–Boston	12	344	134	77	.575	53	23	.755	11	44	0	5	27	194	16.2
1982-83–Boston	7	177	62	34	.548	18	10	.556	5	16	0	3	7	78	11.1
1983-84–Boston	23	702	244	123	.504	121	94	.777	27	75	1	3	35	340	14.8
1984-85–Boston	21	873	303	172	.568	150	121	.807	32	73	3	13	46	465	22.1
1985-86–Boston	18	715	290	168	.579	141	112	.794	48	64	0	8	43	448	24.9
Totals........	98	3071	1146	635	.554	519	400	.771	137	323	5	36	183	1670	17.0

Three-Point Field Goals: 1982-83, 0-1; 1983-84, 0-3; 1985-86, 0-1. *Totals*: 0-5

MICHAEL JORDAN

University of North Carolina Record

Year	G.	Min.	FGA	FGM	Pct.	FTA	FTM	Pct.	Reb.	Pts.
81-82	34	.....	358	191	.534	108	78	.722	149	469
82-83	36	.....	527	182	.535	167	123	.737	197	721
83-84	31	.....	448	247	.551	145	113	.779	163	607
Totals	101		1333	720	.540	420	314	.748	509	1788

Three-Point Field Goals: 1982-83, 34-for-76 (.447).

NBA Regular Season Record

Season–Team	G.	Min.	FGA	FGM	Pct.	FTA	FTM	Pct.	Ast.	PF	Dq.	Stl.	Blk.	Pts.
84-85–Chicago	82	3144	1625	837	.515	746	630	.845	481	285	4	196	69	2313
85-86–Chicago	18	451	328	150	.457	125	105	.840	53	46	0	37	21	408
Totals	100	3595	1953	987	.505	871	735	.844	534	331	4	234	90	2721

Three-Point Field Goals: 1984-85, 9-for-52 (.173); 1985-86, 3-for-18 (.167). Totals: 12-for-70 (.171).

NBA Play-off Stats

	G.	Min.	FGA	FGM.	Pct.	FTA	FTM	Pct.	Ast.	PF	Dq.	Stl.	Blk.	Pts.	Avg
1984-85–Chicago	4	171	78	34	.436	58	48	.828	34	15	0	11	4	117	29.3
1985-86–Chicago	3	135	95	48	.505	39	34	.872	17	13	1	7	4	130	43.3
Totals	7	306	173	82	.474	97	82	.845	51	28	1	18	8	247	35.3

The author wishes to acknowledge the following:

Steve Thompson, the Basketball Hall of Fame

The Sporting News

Sports Illustrated magazine

Paul A. McHale

Ebony magazine

Susan Licata

ProServ

Doug Besen

Tom Greenhoe, Assistant SID, University of Minnesota